NFL TEAM STORIES

THE STORY OF THE

LOS ANGELES CHARGERS

By K.C. Kelley

Kaleidoscope
Minneapolis, MN

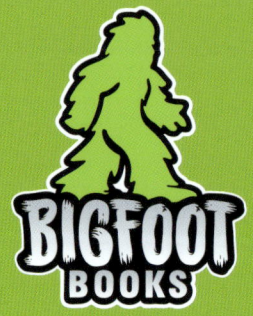

The Quest for Discovery Never Ends

....

This edition first published in 2021 by Kaleidoscope Publishing, Inc.

No part of this publication may be reproduced in whole or in part without written permission of the publisher.

For information regarding permission, write to
Kaleidoscope Publishing, Inc.
6012 Blue Circle Drive
Minnetonka, MN 55343

Library of Congress Control Number
2020936003

ISBN
978-1-64519-234-3 (library bound)
978-1-64519-302-9 (ebook)

Text copyright © 2021 by Kaleidoscope Publishing, Inc. All-Star Sports, Bigfoot Books, and associated logos are trademarks and/or registered trademarks of Kaleidoscope Publishing, Inc.

Printed in the United States of America.

FIND ME IF YOU CAN!

Bigfoot lurks within one of the images in this book. It's up to you to find him!

TABLE OF CONTENTS

Kickoff!	4
Chapter 1: Chargers History	6
Chapter 2: Chargers All-Time Greats	16
Chapter 3: Chargers Superstars	22
Beyond the Book	28
Research Ninja	29
Further Resources	30
Glossary	31
Index	32
Photo Credits	32
About the Author	32

KICKOFF!

Keee-rack!

The sound of a lightning bolt splits the air. The bright flash lights up the sky. A bolt like that is the symbol of the Los Angeles Chargers. They try to strike like lightning against other NFL teams. The team is still looking for its first Super Bowl title. When will that lightning strike? Let's meet the Chargers!

FUN FACT

The Chargers' team name comes from the bugle call, "Charge!"

Chapter 1
Chargers History

Barron Hilton owned a lot of hotels. He wanted to own an NFL team, too. No one would sell him one. So he and some other rich men started a new league. The American Football League (AFL) began in 1960. Hilton's team was the Los Angeles Chargers. The next year, Hilton moved his team to San Diego.

In 10 seasons, the Chargers played for the AFL title five times. They won it all in 1963. (See page 14.) In 1970, the Chargers and nine other AFL teams joined the NFL.

FUN FACT
Take a good guess at what hotels the Hilton family owns!

Barron Hilton (far right)

7

Don Coryell became the Chargers coach in 1979. He brought a new type of offense called "Air Coryell." That was because Coryell made the Chargers into a passing team. Most teams did more runs than passes. Coryell changed that.

San Diego became a great passing team. Coryell called for long **bombs** and lots of short passes. His team made the playoffs four years in a row. Fans thrilled at the exciting, high-scoring games. Quarterback Dan Fouts led the way for Air Coryell.

Don Coryell

Dan Fouts

Natrone Means scored in Super Bowl XXIX.

The 1994 Chargers nearly became champions. They won 11 games and made the playoffs. Stan Humphries connected with Mark Seay for a short TD pass late in the first playoff game. San Diego beat Miami 22–21. In the AFC Championship Game, the defense came through. Led by Junior Seau, San Diego won 17–13.

The Chargers made it to their first Super Bowl! They fought hard, but lost to San Francisco 49–26.

San Diego was sad after the Super Bowl.

From 2004 to 2009, the Chargers made the playoffs five of six seasons. A big reason was "L.T." LaDainian Tomlinson was a touchdown machine. He led the Chargers in rushing nine times. In 2006, he set an NFL record with 31 total TDs! L.T. spun through defenders and sprinted for the **end zone**!

In 2017, the team moved back to where it started. As of 2020, the Los Angeles Chargers took the field in the brand-new SoFi Stadium.

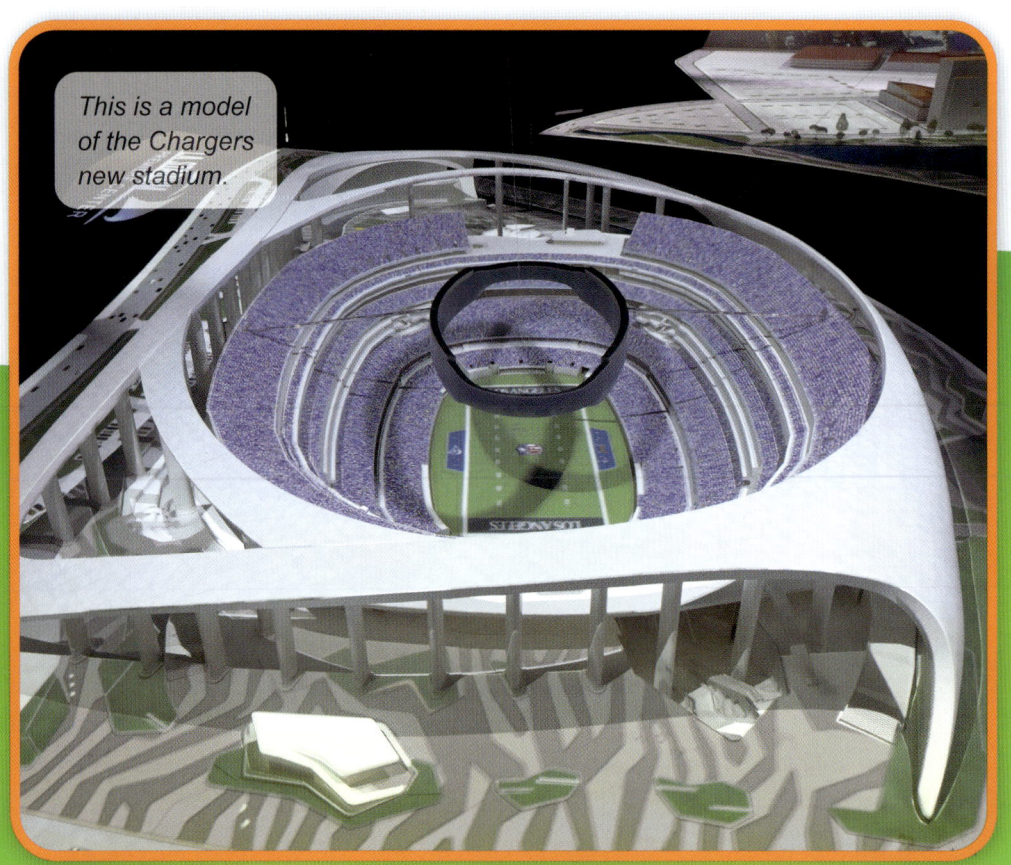

This is a model of the Chargers new stadium.

TIMELINE OF THE LOS ANGELES CHARGERS

1960
1960: Los Angeles Chargers begin play.

1961
1961: Chargers move to San Diego.

1963
1963: Chargers win AFL championship.

1994
1994: Chargers play in Super Bowl XXIX.

2007
2007: Chargers reach AFC Championship Game.

2017
2017: Chargers move back to Los Angeles.

2018
2018: Chargers return to playoffs under coach Anthony Lynn.

CHAMPIONS!

The 1963 Boston Patriots had a very good defense. The team gave up the second-fewest points in the AFL. The Chargers did not care. In the AFL Championship Game, San Diego put on an offensive show!

The Chargers scored three TDs in the first quarter. The highlight came when running back Paul Lowe rambled 58 yards to the end zone.

Boston rallied to make the score 24–10. Then San Diego really turned on the gas. QB Tobin Rote threw three TD passes in the second half. One was to future Hall of Famer Lance Alworth for 48 yards. QB John Hadl capped off the scoring with a one-yard run.

The final score was a scoreboard-breaker—Chargers 51, Patriots 10.

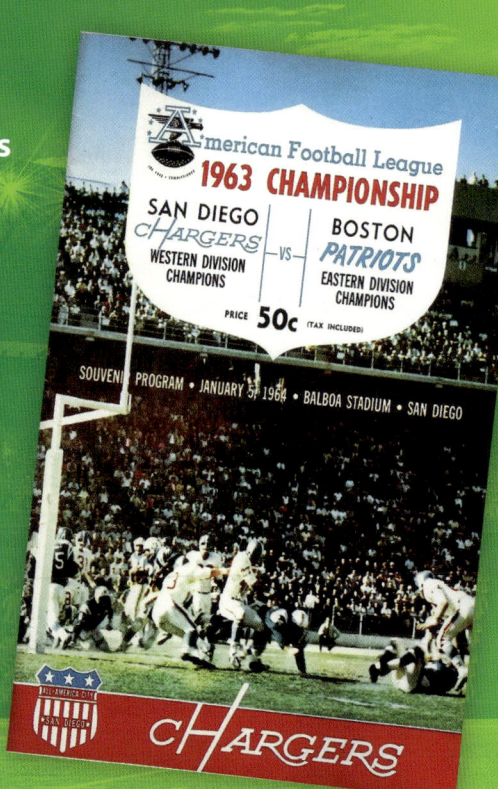

A poster for the 1963 AFL title game.

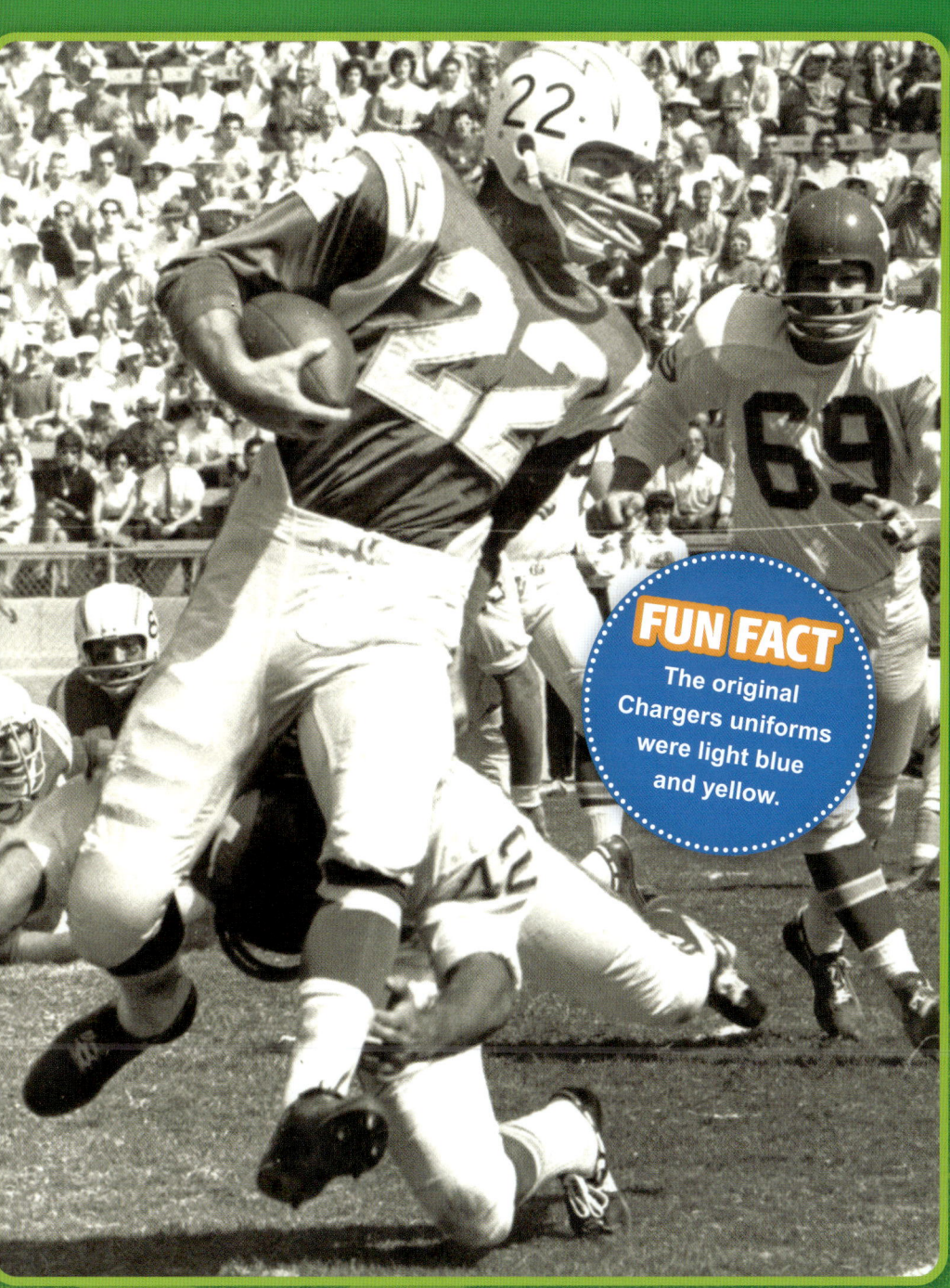

FUN FACT
The original Chargers uniforms were light blue and yellow.

Chapter 2
Chargers All-Time Greats

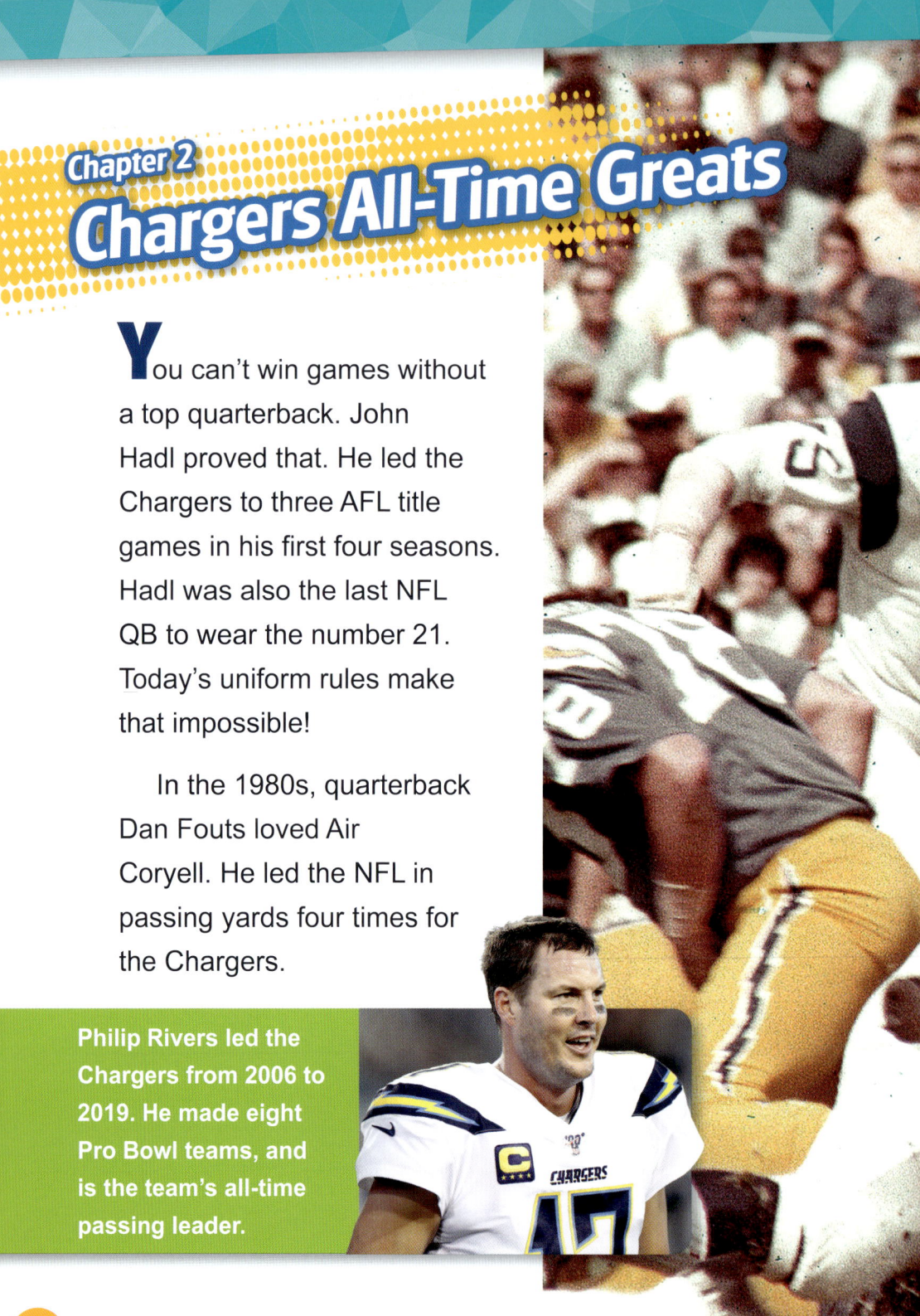

You can't win games without a top quarterback. John Hadl proved that. He led the Chargers to three AFL title games in his first four seasons. Hadl was also the last NFL QB to wear the number 21. Today's uniform rules make that impossible!

In the 1980s, quarterback Dan Fouts loved Air Coryell. He led the NFL in passing yards four times for the Chargers.

Philip Rivers led the Chargers from 2006 to 2019. He made eight Pro Bowl teams, and is the team's all-time passing leader.

John Hadl (21)

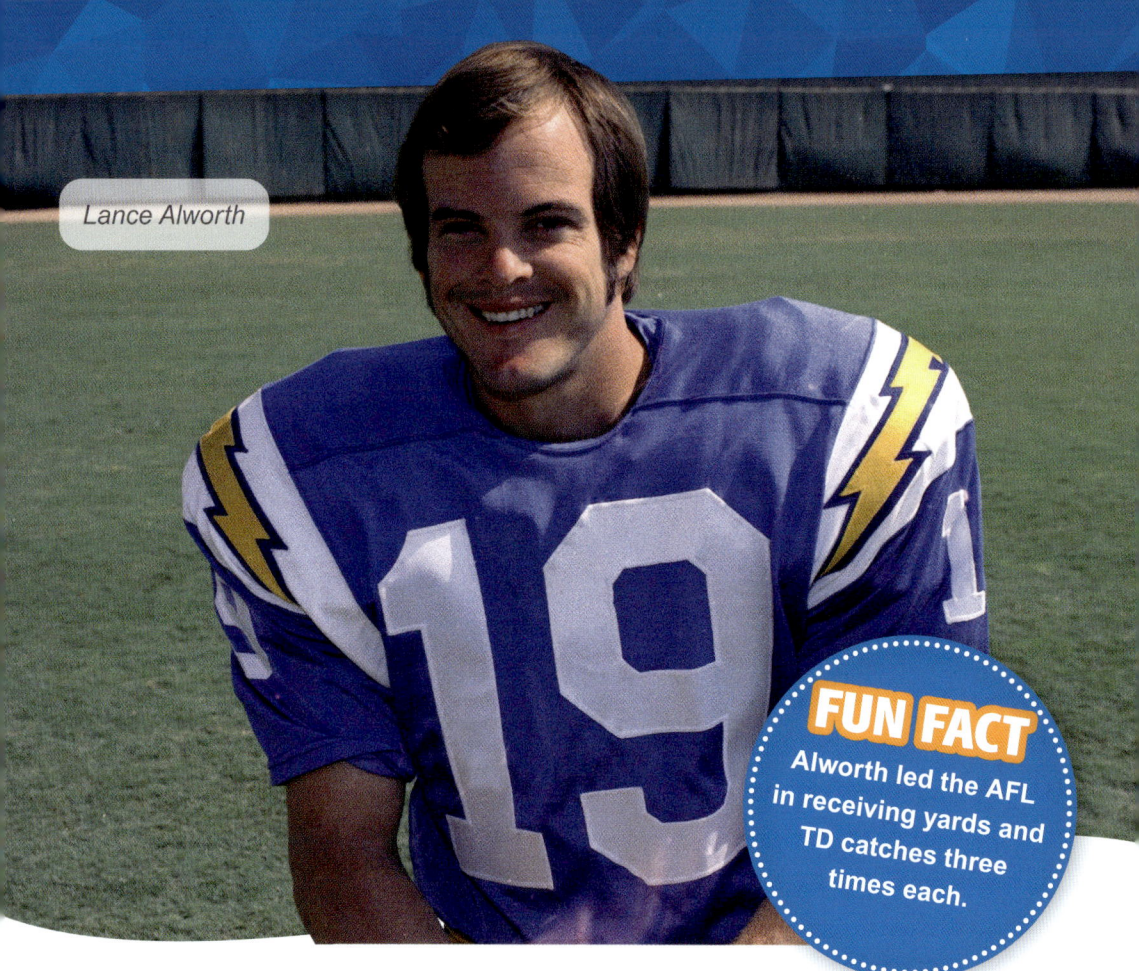

Lance Alworth

FUN FACT
Alworth led the AFL in receiving yards and TD catches three times each.

Bambi caught a lot of passes for the Chargers. No, that was not the cartoon deer. Bambi was the nickname of star receiver Lance Alworth. He was fast and could leap high for passes. Later, Charlie Joiner was the team's star pass-catcher. He and Fouts combined for highlight after highlight.

Antonio Gates was a top basketball player in college. Instead of the NBA, he chose to join the NFL. As a tight end, he went to eight **Pro Bowls**. He'll be in the Hall of Fame someday, too.

Antonio Gates

LaDainian Tomlinson could do it all. He scored 153 touchdowns for San Diego. He had 15 receptions TDs and ran for 138. L.T. was one of the most **dominant** runners in the NFL in the 2000s. He was named the NFL Most Valuable Player in 2006.

His best game came against the Raiders. They were a big **rival** for the Chargers. In a 2003 game, he rambled for 243 yards against the Raiders. The Chargers won, thanks to L.T.'s skills!

LaDainian Tomlinson

CHARGERS
RECORDS

These players piled up the best stats in Chargers history. The numbers are career records through the 2019 season.

Total TDs: LaDainian Tomlinson, 153

TD Passes: Philip Rivers, 397

Passing Yards: Philip Rivers, 59,271

Receiving Yards: Antonio Gates, 11,841

Rushing Yards: LaDainian Tomlinson, 12,490

Receptions: Antonio Gates, 955

Points: John Carney, 1,076

Sacks: Leslie O'Neal, 105.5

Chapter 3
Chargers Superstars

Tyrod Taylor proves that hanging in there pays off. Taylor joined the NFL in 2011. He was a backup in Baltimore for four seasons. In 2015, he moved to Buffalo. He was the starter there for three seasons. He showed off a strong arm. Taylor was also a very good runner. Best of all, he rarely threw interceptions.

But then the Bills let him go in 2017. He spent a year in Cleveland and didn't play much. In 2019, he backed up Philip Rivers in San Diego.

In 2020, he'll be "the man" for the Chargers. Taylor's patience and skill have landed him a great opportunity. Chargers fans hope he can come through!

The Chargers boast a solid running game. The main runner is Austin Ekeler. He is small and quick. Ekeler is also great at catching passes. He gives the Chargers a two-way threat on offense.

Austin Ekeler

Keenan Allen

Rivers has made Keenan Allen his main target. Allen has caught at least 97 passes in three seasons. He is especially good at finding space across the middle of the field.

FUN FACT
Joey Bosa's younger brother, Nick, is a star pass-rusher for the 49ers.

Joey Bosa

When the Chargers are on defense, Joey Bosa is the boss. Using power and speed, Bosa **sacks** QBs. He had at least 10.5 sacks in three seasons. On running plays, he makes sure no one gets past him!

On passing plays, Bosa gets help from Casey Hayward. This defensive back attracts footballs. He led the NFL in interceptions in 2016. Few receivers find open space against this veteran.

Together, all these Chargers hope to bring a Super Bowl to the team's new home.

BEYOND
THE BOOK

After reading the book, it's time to think about what you learned. Try the following exercises to jumpstart your ideas.

RESEARCH

FIND OUT MORE. Where would you go to find out more about your favorite NFL teams and players? Check out NFL.com, of course. Each team also has its own website. What other sports information sites can you find? See if you can find other cool facts about your favorite team.

CREATE

GET ARTISTIC. Each NFL team has a logo. The Chargers logo shows a lightning bolt. Get some art materials and try designing your own Chargers logo. Or create a new team and make a logo for it. What colors would you choose? How would you draw a mascot?

DISCOVER

GO DEEP! As this book shows, the Chargers are moving into a new stadium in 2020. Have you ever moved? What was it like? How did you have to get used to a new place? What advice would you give Chargers players as they get used to their new home?

GROW

GET OUT AND PLAY! You don't need to be in the NFL to enjoy football. You just need a football and some friends. Play touch or tag football. Or you can hang cloth flags from your belt; grab the belt and make the "tackle." See who has the best arm to be quarterback. Who is the best receiver? Who can run the fastest? Time to play football!

RESEARCH NINJA

Visit *www.ninjaresearcher.com/2343* to learn how to take your research skills and book report writing to the next level!

RESEARCH

DIGITAL LITERACY TOOLS

SEARCH LIKE A PRO
Learn about how to use search engines to find useful websites.

FACT OR FAKE?
Discover how you can tell a trusted website from an untrustworthy resource.

TEXT DETECTIVE
Explore how to zero in on the information you need most.

SHOW YOUR WORK
Research responsibly— learn how to cite sources.

WRITE

GET TO THE POINT
Learn how to express your main ideas.

PLAN OF ATTACK
Learn prewriting exercises and create an outline.

DOWNLOADABLE REPORT FORMS

Further Resources

BOOKS

Gigliotti, Jim. *Philip Rivers: Football Players Making a Difference*. Minneapolis: Bearport Publishing, 2016.

Kelley, K.C. *2020 Football Superstars*. Santa Barbara, Calif: Beach Ball Books, 2020.

Whiting, Jim. *Los Angeles Chargers: NFL Today*. Minneapolis: North Star Editions, 2019.

WEBSITES

FACTSURFER

Factsurfer.com gives you a safe, fun way to find more information.

1. Go to www.factsurfer.com.
2. Enter "Los Angeles Chargers" into the search box and click 🔍
3. Select your book cover to see a list of related websites.

Glossary

bombs: very long passes. Fouts aimed a 60-yard bomb at Joiner.

dominant: the most powerful or successful. The Chargers were dominant in passing during the Air Coryell years.

end zone: the area at each end of the field in which touchdowns are scored. Tomlinson burst into the end zone for six points!

Pro Bowl: the NFL's annual all-star game, held after the season. Fouts played well enough to earn a spot in six Pro Bowls.

rival: a very close and fierce opponent. The Chargers probably look at the Raiders as their biggest rivals.

sacks: tackles made on the quarterback behind the line of scrimmage. Seau celebrated loudly after all of his sacks.

Index

"Air Coryell," 8, 16
Allen, Keenan, 25
Alworth, Lance, 14, 18
American Football League (AFL), 6, 14, 16
Baltimore Ravens, 22
Bosa, Joey, 27
Boston Patriots, 14
Buffalo Bills, 22
Coryell, Don, 8
Ekeler, Austin, 24
Fouts, Dan, 8, 16, 18
Gates, Antonio, 18
Hadl, John, 14, 16
Hayward, Casey, 27
Hilton, Barron, 6
Humphries, Stan, 11
Joiner, Charlie, 18
Lowe, Paul, 14
Oakland Raiders, 20
Rivers, Philip, 22, 25
Rote, Tobin, 14
Seau, Junior, 11
Seay, Mark, 11
SoFi Stadium, 12
Super Bowl, 4, 11, 27
Taylor, Tyrod, 22
Tomlinson, LaDainian "L.T.," 12, 20

PHOTO CREDITS

The images in this book are reproduced through the courtesy of: AP Images: Pro Football Hall of Fame 6; Chuck Solomon 8; Al Messerschmidt 10, 18; Lenny Ingelzi 11; Kirby Lee 12; 14; NFL Photos 16. Focus on Football: 19, 20, 24, 25, 26. Newscom: Kevin Abele/Icon SW 22. SPG: 14 inset. Shutterstock: Thomas Ramsauer 4. **Cover photo:** Focus on Football.

About the Author

K.C. Kelley is the author of more than 100 sports books for kids. He has written about football, baseball, basketball, soccer, and many other popular games. He lives in Santa Barbara, California, with his family.